BODY OF RENDER

Body of Render

poems

Felicia Zamora

2018
Red Hen Press
BENJAMIN SALTMAN
AWARD

 Red Hen Press | *Pasadena, CA*

Library of Congress Cataloging-in-Publication Data

Names: Zamora, Felicia M., author.
Title: Body of render : poems / Felicia Zamora.
Description: Pasadena, CA : Red Hen Press, [2020]
Identifiers: LCCN 2019036889 | ISBN 9781597099752 (trade paperback)
Subjects: LCSH: Human rights—Poetry. | Marginality, Social—United
States—Poetry. | LCGFT: Poetry.
Classification: LCC PS3626.A6278 B63 2020 | DDC 811/.6—dc23
LC record available at https://lccn.loc.gov/2019036889

The National Endowment for the Arts, the Los Angeles County Arts Commission, the Ahman-
son Foundation, the Dwight Stuart Youth Fund, the Max Factor Family Foundation, the Pasa-
dena Tournament of Roses Foundation, the Pasadena Arts & Culture Commission and the City
of Pasadena Cultural Affairs Division, the City of Los Angeles Department of Cultural Affairs,
the Audrey & Sydney Irmas Charitable Foundation, the Kinder Morgan Foundation, the Meta
& George Rosenberg Foundation, the Allergan Foundation, the Riordan Foundation, Amazon
Literary Partnership, and the Mara W. Breech Foundation partially support Red Hen Press.

First Edition
Published by Red Hen Press
www.redhen.org

ACKNOWLEDGMENTS

Gratitude goes to the entire team at Red Hen Press, specifically Kate Gale who believed in this book, Natasha McClellan, and Tobi Harper for letting this book breathe and live in this world.

Heartfelt gratitude to Marilyn Nelson for selecting this manuscript to win the Benjamin Saltman Award, as I am forever honored my words made an impression. Gratitude to Maggie Smith and TC Tolbert for speaking to my poetry and this book.

My sincere gratitude to the editors and editorial teams of the following journals and presses in which these poems first appeared, sometimes in different forms. Your hard work and dedication to the literary world helps artists bring their creations to the world. *Alaska Quarterly Review*, "Of mouth this heavenly body"; *azcentral.com*, "In the light of"; *Birdfeast*, "Loose Clench" and "In the month of not-so-thankful thoughts"; *Denver Quarterly*, "Comfort in knowing that mathematically you are not alone in choice of love over hate," "Mathematics of healing: a poem to America," "Sores & Dressings: *A Post Election Moment of Comfort*"; *Dusie*, "Heliocentric"; *Foundry*, "Love bold"; *Green Mountains Review*, "In our bundle"; *Lana Turner*, "The retreat," "In search of feminism," "Once you lie a lot, it's like second nature," and "Ghost of innocence"; *New Limestone Review*, "This wild in which we"; *Nine Mile Magazine*, "If starlight be"; *OmniVerse*, "In the make," "At the hand of other," "America, ain't I a woman," "Winterize, oh America," and "In time, brave, brave"; *Poetrybay*, "& in unmake, reveal"; *Tarpaulin Sky*, "Poem to America [My nerves expose, unwilling;]"; *The Collagist*, "In our nation's capital" [& what releases from your body...]; *West Branch* (Contemporary American Prose Poetry Feature), "Unapologetic," and "In preparation for fiery climates: a poem to America"; *wildness*, "& in burn you also" and "Star in burn"; *Zocalo Public Square*, "Back to quiet."

Thank you to Tupelo Press's 30/30 Project in which first drafts of thirty of these poems were first generated in November 2016.

My heart and deepest gratitude go out to my family, friends, and communities: Melody Henderson, Joe Zamora, Linda Zamora, Shahida Robinson, Melinda Van Rooyen, Justin Petropoulos, Malik Toms, John Calderazzo, Stephanie G'Schwind, Dan Beachy-Quick, Todd Mitchell, Beth and Bruce Van Wyk, Tammy and Mark Van Maurer, Michelle Deschenes, Susan Harness, Heather Matthews, and Foula Dimopoulos. My art would not be possible without your enduring support and belief in me as a human being. I am forever grateful for all of you. The magic you all bring to my life is unfathomable. Gracias. Gracias.

Chris, always. Always us. Our journeys of the elation and the horrid, always us, my love. Always us.

Finally, lovely reader, here we are together. How can we not be? These words are for us.

for you, lovely reader . . . for us

Contents

RAW DELIBERATION OF CIRCUMSTANCES

NO APOLOGIES TO AMERICA ANYMORE

INFINITE DESIGN OF A MOUTH, OPEN

Body of Render

Why are we here if not for each other?
　　—Claudia Rankine, *Don't Let Me Be Lonely*

We, too, can divide ourselves, it's true.
But only into flesh and a broken whisper.
　　—Wisława Szymbroska, *view with a grain of sand*

Say it again—we are
spared nothing.
　　—Yusef Komunyakaa, *I Apologize for the Eyes in My Head*

AT THE HAND OF OTHER

At the hand of other

& of desire; how we thirst below flesh, below
cortex, below pelvis; the minute ticks we
hardly keep at bay; how we often inside out;
how we bells struck & our music resides first
in body, then in {*mindful this gap*}; we bounce
back to ourselves, to lick our own lips & feel
the weight of our own motion & emotion:
jellyfish in change of water's influence; to be
at the hand of other; say *this too, desire*; how
afferent, we, always in lead toward; how we all
nerves in gather, *message message* & our pupils
dilate us; how we all wet & longing, cell to cell.

In our bundle

When we think of sticks, do we think *tree*; *oh bramble of me*; what part of us, scatters wind, becomes home to something other; how your skinny bones in drape, mulberry limbs; *oh slats of light, ribs of*; & dusk always resides in chest, in fissures between lobes where all of us lie temporal & disoriented, *oh this piece of*; suture back; yes a question, *no no* an answer; how skeletal the bark of us, word & flesh; *I left me for you* propped against the girth of trunk; how we shed ourselves over & over: snake bundled in snake skin; once, yes, once we were one.

In fall or other shitty metaphors
for depression

When silence does not exist & the mind
drapes in whispers; a creeping creep; clock
ticks etch the eardrum; fingers to throat; how
lightening   in   passage;   how   all   this
electrification in your chest; cave for sear, in
remembrance *live, live, live*; ribs swell, just
before; a growing presence of plead, *o-h g-o-d*,
syllables strung in temporal lobe; how a world
smells of Marlboros & whiskey & you adverse
to your own life, crawl back into your jaw; &
you lug your torso around on sore hips, *oh wait*
of frost to blanket this dead of fall.

In the light of

Light exists, then, this November light; how
we yellow in the dried, in the plummet; sun,
gorgeous sore, tests the pupil in constrict, lips
in part *more more*; say *alive* & feel it—inside all
these organs & cells, how they animate
together; how we all in animation together; in
tether to the ball of gas in gush 92.96 million
miles from; & earth, say it, *earth*, binds us to
other; say *molecule*; say *seven billion billion billion*;
yes, that's you: body of minuscule bodies; our
matter in constant question, bends in shadow.

Back to quiet

& the blades of grass prepare for dormant; *think think* in stillness, under winter's palm in swift approach; desire now this return to dust, this work beyond autumnal brain, autumnal body; how we plot our birth & death among cycles of seasons, ignoring, at times, dusks & dawns in hurry, in hurry; *oh the yawn of us*; how we tire of tunnels, pupil's capture of the backs of our own hands; all these keyboard strokes; how we ache in our hippocampi; we sift memory in gather, in gentle care, to mind the incessant pull back to elements, back to *quiet*.

In the name of freedom
(an election thought)

What meaning lost in the name of; think *crusades*; what you know of good intentions; when last you brother; when last you sister; how social media invents: a therapy gap to consider less & speak more; when did we become definitive statements behind cyber cyber-degradations; say *this lack of, oh empathy oh*; how we stay at wrist-lengths from society, our keyboard cage; such less *we we*, more *my my*; how disconnection: a sickness we cure with more sickness, more declarations behind closed minds; elections reveal one of our faces—we a nation of; marvelous colors, creeds, identities, ideas; how we in terrifying action to each other; & how the first woman, say *president*, say *qualified*, say *what lovely reality*, must be candidate to: say *sexual predator*, say a *joke's sad fruition*; what cruel reality this historical privilege, this thumb pressed upon you & you &; how some close their eyes; how you will weep, in one way or another.

& in burn you also

The cattails golden in the afternoon's low sun;
smell of dried sap releases in each crunch
under step; here the trees & ground prepare;
say, *smoke of what burns*; how we all carry on
wind in our delicate, our smallness; one must
completely disintegrate before; think *phoenix*;
& you so close to combustion—you long for
anything resembling flame; this dirt path,
travelers before you; how we bind to each
precipice before us; your hand in lover's hand;
how in one moment: a guide, how other: *lost,
so lost* & smoke of the burning fills you.

Election Night

Tonight electoral electoral electoral;
dichotomy of blue & red; how my Latina
body, my pinkish vagina, my nipples protrude,
just so; how blue my lips after blow job; how
blue my veins in loyal pump to heart; how
nasty woman me; how proud; & the nation
teeters on a razor, ready to bleed—*red red red*
my pupils in stun—for a president who
believes me a *disgusting animal*; how numbers
tally & tally & panic seeds in my chest, my
mind traumas, *shit shit*; inauguration ladies, the
president finds you all *beautiful pieces of ass.*

Poem to America

My nerves expose, unwilling; these cells & fibers race in transmit; *oh impulse of me*; skin peeled away, how defense fails; & my eyes, *oh eyes*, in uncontrollable wet; to witness, to experience decimation in the aortic sack; *oh society oh*; what you cull, piece by piece; what you strip; what grows back only in time, *in time*; hold these bones up to the light; do you see me in porous cavities forming despite what torn & torn; my flesh under your claws; from hollow & cold & seamless, I rise; sew this heart anew; I long to forgive you. *Forgive.*

Rise

To all my brothers & sisters of color, Rise; to my gay, trans, queer soulmates, Rise; to all my nasty women, Rise; to all who experience sexual assault, Rise; to the immigrants who make this nation great, Rise; alone is not us; Rise; degradation not our destiny; Rise; hateful slander in tear at our children's ears, tear our hearts, remains feeble to our strength; Rise; *not alone not alone not alone not alone not alone not alone not alone not alone not alone not a lone not alone not alone not alone not alone* not a singular voice left unattended; Rise, yes, Rise!

Survival—three days after election

Tell me story: a story of fields beyond horizon
of skyscrapers of lake over lake of bridges of
bays of swamps; of this story, paint me a heart;
not a symbol red, a meatish, blood-filled organ
with veins & arteries protruding; paint
striations of muscle at apex; what open &
exposed reveal; paint trunk of aorta; *oh aorta oh*
weight you carry in arch to limbs & organs, yet
not the lungs; *not the lungs*—think now how we
breathe after aorta collapses; think now how
we still intake air, still balance, yet bloody; *oh
lungs oh; fill release, fill release, fill release, fill . . .*

Comfort in knowing that mathematically you are not alone in choice of love over hate

If you dissect down the human brain, gelatinous everything & tendrils, fat & pink, hemispheres in fan; think *coral*; how make we; say *mostly water water*; all the flame & mystery lost in faint whisper, *cadaver*; how we inside, yet not; how we parts in shove: organ on top of vein on top of bone; intricate & ephemeral; when you think *my brain*, think *oh uncommon me*; yet your brain & your brain & your brain resemble; we comprise of the same cells, same tissues, & systems; touch your sternum; say *seven billion breastbones*; do the math; exhale.

Not my president

For the next four years, I am a sovereign
nation of one: one mind inside this one body;
my pussy *Hands Off* to a government, not
mine, not for me, not my voice; *oh lovely nasty
estrogen of me*; how I life-raft to other 62 million
sovereign bodies whose vote pleaded *love*; I
pay money to protect the rights & services of,
say *underrepresented*, say *need*, say *who desire love
& peace*; say *taxation* under my breath, this
government, not my government, takes,
elongates gaps & betrays; my nation spells
hate: t-r-u-m-p; my nation: a voice crying out.

Fallacy Catch-22

Prague, 2002: *Sorry, we just can't separate you from your president*; words, words in haunt from the German man in glasses; how cross oceans & seas perceive us; *wait, no, what have we*; your question lingers above in the smog we laden our hearts & bodies with; *1460 days*, count them, *count*; how we did this, & now we must count, must participate; how what's decent fickles at heart's core; & what of truth in memory; what fallacy, the amygdala, if it did indeed harbor the brain's fear, how you'd long to pluck that idea too, shouting *No No No* . . .

In crawl out of cessation

How the aspen trunk settles into its ghost-white bark on a palette of Prussian & Maya blue; how sun silhouettes skeletal branches this final show, this last burn before drag into horizon; how we all in swallow in a belly of; all this accumulation, all this letting go, say *each day, day, day*; what winds your heart in twilight, brings limbs to rise & organs tick; you who were rendered in questions with questions infused in your blood, *oh unanswerable molecule of you; oh inorganic beast; oh organic beast*; burn down, *day day*, then rise.

In time, brave, brave

You must step out—cranium a cave & yes, a
womb, but how your thoughts cavern so; *out
out you* & taste dust comingled in the breeze;
how these lips, chapped & longing, gateway to
voice; do you remember, surge in esophagus
in build, in build; what constructs in the lungs,
in hug of heart, *oh beat of us*, keeps not at bay,
reveals despite our will to tamp; voice braves
us a new, demonstrates us on our behalf,
alludes capture; & how simple this breath, this
gust of air from our ribs; & yet *out* we must go
to meet other's voices, yes, say *voices*, because
alone is not we; alone in skull before—*leap*.

Restroom hug

& in a space so common, a simple phrase; *I
am so proud of you*, a woman, a colleague in the
restroom reaches her arms toward you,
around you; what *embrace* means; to feel, yes
feel, arms on arms & hands on your back; how
gentle of gentle; to linger in moment—to be
in a field of lilacs, say *oh sun peck these cheekbones
& chin bones, oh* & the heat of you collapses
in breeze & the two smell of one—here, inside
skull, in industrial room of tiles & metal, you
melt into the body of a stranger; let fear slide
down your throat to stomach pit; let lull, lull.

What the world offers

Outside the coffee shop five Twizzlers half-
squish into cement; how half-red beautifully
braided & half-red flattened, blood-like to run
only into a waxy shell; what textures & un-
textures abound; think *exactly*, for today that's
you, under sole; sole unaware you exist except
in brief moment when you interrupt gait, mid-
trample, ever so, ever so; how air exhausts you
& your organs gel porously into one another;
& you think *stay down, let rubber & elements wipe
you*; instead you stroke new dimensions, laugh
& peel chest, again, off what the world offers.

Sores & Dressings: *A Post Election Moment of Comfort*

You rub fingers to fingers & *yes*, both right
& left belong to you; a comfort, today, burrows
in the crevasses of jaw, thighs, spinal column;
flesh bit, a sore in gape, once bloody now
swollen lumps the underfold of your lip; you
tongue space between tooth & chin, *tongue &*
tongue, innocent & childlike & the taste where
pain once was—vanished, yet lingers, ghosts;
what do you really know of wound, of heal,
of abilities to; this body dresses you & how
bone carries organs, organs blood, blood cells
& all this tethers to a mind in float; *yes, float.*

The snowman

Recall; *no*; you don't remember building snowmen; in stand over your nephew's work: blueberry eyes, carrot nose, pine cone buttons in set of three; what we think we know & what we only imagine; you scoop the grittiness, the debris clustered pockets of ice & feel the surge rush through your palms; *never too late* & hands in pack; how simple this r/evolution on this, say *rounded plane,* say *mother mother,* oh ball you bound in gravity; & in moment, we look around, weightless & bewildered; & how light bends leaner in November's autumnal; *see, see.*

Love bold

When you first learned *other*, you a target of
slurs & fingers of small fists in shove; *other*
always *always* lives internal; *other* bunks in
between each disc in your vertebral column,
each   gland   you   salivate   from,   each
constriction   of   pupil   in   search   of
understanding; *other* finds home in tendrils of
brain, safe behind skull; think *walls*, think *what*
walls keep, what walls inhibit; how you no
prisoner & thus, *out out brave other*, into a world
that throws stones, a world that beats &
batters; how you, *other*, love bold, love bold.

In the month of not-so-thankful thoughts

Crumpled in over & over; how this lacquer &
metal: a wad violently prepared for discard;
what *collision* resembles; & her cheeks tuck
tight into your collarbone; her staccato breath
heaves; the smell of her hair; her body in slow
between your arms & *thankful* evolves, beyond
a word, beyond a word you take for granted
until this moment, now, when her face in your
neck; & *sister* a cellular construct in swell inside
your aortic sack; pupils gather the scene where
debris litters; pieces of engine where a body is
not; knot of you, in gradual unwind, folds so.

Character beyond definition

You cry today; & how your brow furrows to
admit the word *cry* in a poem; think *oh hate of
use, this abstract definer such as "hate"*; yet, word
in construct of letter tumbling after letter,
exemplifies itself as word; & if we all designed
with purpose in mind, think *lucky to be useful,*
oh alphabet how you conjure our witness;
today your pupils absorb the sun in slice
between clouds this late late afternoon; feel
November's sharp wind on scalp & think, *oh,
word, oh* to define purpose; how all these
characters disobey, at the loveliest moment.

On words: a Thanksgiving thought

The power lines flutter, chatter of energy &
trains roar below, parallel in sound & motion;
this day wraps itself in a word, say *holiday*;
how jaws & tongue work to bring our
thoughts to fruition; what lovely imagination
dwells in our mouths; & the word, say *holiday*,
embodies, too, this capacity for power; no
wonder we feed where we speak; how
delicious this act of convection from brain
down to trachea; from the hollow of us, acts
reverberate; & so our limbs animate to hug
our loved ones, bake our pies, *chatter, chatter.*

In the make

In breath, you rise from your own esophagus;
& how in thought of the word, the larynx
prepares; you don't remember when thoughts
steadied themselves in your throat, bricks
built; how a child climbs out of cave, squints
toward sun, say, *how bright as bright me*; our
innocence compacts in molars & jaw clicks;
say *how build me*; little fists scaffold the
epiglottis; the voice of you: *want want want* &
in the chant, the build, the rise; how structure
& formulation burrow us & we absolute & full
of holes in the make, in the gape.

Star in burn

Against night's crisp envelop, your heart weighs against the stars; how you simply organs in surround by one membrane of flesh, one membrane of atmosphere; & farther still, exhaustive quiet of space; think *how alone & never alone you always & never*; 25 trillion miles beyond your ribs, three stars bind together in gravity's tight hug; whisper *Alpha Centauri* & water vapor releases, say *moist lungs*, say *oh energy generation*; how a body keeps molecules in motion, in pack; say *how gas evolves & heart a pump*; you ball of gas, star in burn, in consume.

Heliocentric

Consider the number of atoms in the human
body; now say *seven billion billion billion*, think
27 zeros as round & contracting as your pupil
in stare at the midday sky; most hydrogen,
oxygen, carbon; *oh elements of you*; consider
Archimedes' *The Sand Reckoner*; what powers
of myriad myriad system; think *M*, think *all the
mathematical symbols & what each represents*; to
count the grains of sand fitted into a universe;
scour your flesh, cells; what do you represent;
think *astrology*; & you, in early winter sun think
yourself: *just a simple grain in tilt, grain in orbit.*

America, ain't I a woman

See my purplish-brownish vagina; how you
say my body one thing; *define not by passage alone*;
estrogen, *oh estrogen*, how what develops me,
unrequited so—*fuck you & all your regulations*;
yell with me, *one hormone does not a human make*;
however you dice me up: through my heart to
medulla oblongata to cerebrum in crowd of
skull, my core resides in electrical impulses,
say *waves waves waves*, not your amber-bullshit
grain *{not about/about you, America}*, in sparks,
thoughts, uncollectable, all me categorization
alludes; so *yes, I am*, & really *fucking yes I am*.

Winterize, oh America

All the trees complete their shed & shrug
what summer left in hurried whimsy; say *you too form
a type of rot*; how we all skeletal in the waning
light of autumn; how the sun bores &
illuminates, say *core of us*; in mesh of branch
tips, a nest, batters late November gusts; how
we must understand abandonment in this late
hour; how we must endure the frigid, the slap;
& a deep & cold tide readies in our hearts,
prepares to lick our wounds in salted shame;
& how American is not unlike a season: vast
& brutal & unforgiving & wondrous to a fault.

Voice witness, *yes, voice*

Let voice permeate, from belly lining to spinal
column; linger, brief, at epiglottis before leap;
oh what body draws; this breath to word; carve
out inside you, tunnels & windpipes; *sing despite
brutality*; what makes us, *oh elements of,* converge
in instrument, heard we must; how nation
yells, beats its chest; & you lovely flag-
burners, you lovely protestors, you lovely
queer & colorful & disabled & un-
documented by bell of voice: *voice*; you brave
throat; voice witness for safe, for other; voice
witness of all love-full; *voice, yes, voice.*

Raw deliberation of circumstances

This wild in which we

& the solitude of the snow leopard atop the Himalayan Mountains; to search connection in the scent of rock faces, in urine of another; how we define singular by relation to plural; a bellow when instinctual gather must occur.

∞

Air, less thin here & yet; we obsess with uniqueness, with boundaries we chunk ourselves into partitions: nations, politics, cities, races, religions; we in awe of walls, of structure; fireflies in pull—of jars over our own heads—in stunt of.

Another snow leopard answers the female's call; & what seclusion bores deep into a being; claws distend & the leopards attack to near death; & of learned violence in this mating scene; how survival changes in distort of.

∞

What we understand of *world* behind glass; say *observer*; we tinker with otherness, securely in our jars; think *distance of you*; how in our chromosomes: a code still carves inside us, longs for interaction; what & how we prepare for.

& in the Andes Mountains, 4,000 meters above, a colony of flamingos; legs freeze into the lake each night; how what we endure becomes a landscape of us; in sun-stroked thaw, a parade of pink; *beak after beak after beak* held high.

∞

How in species, say *oh our delicate humanity*, the lovely of gather; how we better in other; say *the we* of we; & all jars stifle our breath, the voice of us in muffle across barriers of our own making; let us unmake in instinct, say *parade parade*.

The retreat

Inside the circle of seventy people; inside a cage
of ribs, your lungs tick in spasmodic rhythm; *heave*
your chest repeats over & over, a hymn of sorts
& you, atheist, in pretend that *belief* ever calmed
anything; outside the panes, snow pummels
the mountain range, sidewalks, the air so crisp
you choke on its necessity; & the room builds
a ladder of terms with no destination: *privilege,*
identity, socialization, liberation, biracial, horizontal
oppression, justice; you pluck them from each breath
to stow each away; how you fear your own
memory a sieve, separating the fine parts &
loose matter of you; how you always in assembly
& deconstruction; this cycle in force *& you are?*
How you came to facilitate, yet, *yet*, this discussion
tears away pieces of you; & someone says *white-*
passing; & how a familiar voice eludes, *not brown*
enough again, *not white enough* again, & your mind
dives back into his words, *you dirty little spic*; how
he, of all people, designed in blood to love you;
& the fear & the small hands in push of your
small body; how you always told *other other*; how
spit saved for you, how knuckles cut on your
cheekbones; how, yes, you Latina & . . . the word

white lingers in your temporal lobe in search of
meaning thrown toward you, again; how violence
so simply stated; & two words in weight, unravel
your identity, here, in space with strangers, your
mind chants *I am enough, I am enough, enough; enough.*

In search of feminism

Your ass, half in, half out of cramp; the conference-
chair routine; *now visualize . . . you, twenty years from . . .*
& the voice in slide down your spinal cord; how you
always in ask: *Next? Next? Next?* Think of the Blue Jay
how she'd starve to death in such linger; how at Edinburgh
Castle, the guard's thick accent, *Am I a fucking parrot?*
in repeat on your approach to Mel & Joe with heads
in nod, in nod; how we don't understand what we don't;
& now, you relax your jaw to ride a beam of light into
your subconscious . . . 'cause? 'cause you didn't get the drift
'cause the new buzz term for *drift* is *glass cliff*; how ceilings,
you know, too easy; we need real-bodily-harm scenarios;
how for thousands of years, someone labeled your vagina
lesser; how someone said, *& this is not for you; this is not
for you; this is not*—draw a line to horizon, a line of society ready
to slap & your face poorly prepared; how exhaustion resembles
your brain, your heart, only 80% of the time; you think
of Woolf; how you always think of Woolf; so you workshop
feminism, you dialogue social justice, you in therapy; *yes
doctor, rage due to election results; yes doctor, being nasty
comforts*; you type *you* so much—this litany makes you
ill; how we turn inside to fight for equity; let's say
society: a house & your body the attic; *yes, yes, build
first*; & if a house in burn; what of you in the attic

flooded with questions; first you sleuth *these cells, our calcium*
what-nots, look around, get to know your guts; then . . .
how lovely *then*; how *first* implies *second*; how steps construct
a gait, a journey; & the journey miles over miles; you fidget
in wait; how Woolf tethers poetry to intellectual freedom
to material things; *yes Woolf, poverty of women requires a room,*
"a room of one's own" & you of all know to leave this room, we
must; & a voice bellows deep in your lungs, in expansion;
& you, on the verge, crawl up & up.

Speak, despite

How to speak; speak difficult, say *race a relation*
how overt & aghast the middles of, say *hate & love*;
when *other* cores you; & you never an apple; not
anyone's cherry; yet the teeth marks you bare;
how *witness* carves you out of spinal cord, a rib
cage, a heart in tired beat; when *witness* grows
in proteins & keratins out your fingernails; say
my claws, my claws; say *you animal, you*; & all times
you've been fingered: agony of sexual assault/
ecstasy of your lover's touch; how we never one
singular anything; how we bare & bare; the white
predator, *be brave, please*, say *rapist*; how you form
thoughts careful now, in bulk before; the *rapist*
entered you, forced dominion over, *recall must must*,
your sleeping body; when *fear* & *rage*, inadequate
words you find yourself torn open from, propel
you to speak out of dream: say *don't tell me how
my strength alarms you*; say *speak, despite, yes, speak.*

Once you lie a lot, it's like second nature

Yes, your partner suffers & all parts
of the word: *alcohol, ism, ic* tumble
out of you; why must you write . . . say
this down, in odd conjure—conversation
you know bound only to impulses
tightly tendriled behind a cranium; in
your peripherals, the gray-haired woman
with back to you; how your heart, oh
this organ in bulky absorption, asks *be*
mother for just this moment; how nothing
brief in distance of separation; strange this
stranger growing in you: what protrudes
in spaces between—inside us striated,
molecules, secrets & shame; how wide
open disclosure's weight, this creation in
broken permutations; say *oh, tongue in lie;*
in permeates us, as us; how to navigate
this full-empty of body; transparent
soul occupying the crevasses, seeding; soul
in spore behind layers of complex cellular
arrangements, yet must now . . . say *tend*
for convenience, say *render*, for lack of.

Of mouth this heavenly body

Paint my tongue cerulean blue
& all that flows from open jaws

transforms into a field of stars
in illumination; how we bind; say

luminous dwarf, say *my galaxy*; how light
fools us; how in space, the hot of hot

burn blue; & every star a sun, every
ray a tongue; say *black body of stars*

in absorb of all; say *electromagnetic
radiation* as if to taste the blaze

of heaven; *oh star,* how you emit
back, swallow unbound & gift & gift,

you gift; *oh celestial body in glow* & so,
too, a mouth in deep open, in expose.

If starlight be

If starlight be how visible & electromagnetic your
form; & all the parts of the unseen we take for granted;
decisions on Capitol Hill spoken into law without say
of anyone other than, say *elected official*, say *O radiation of*
you lost behind another broken system; say *we made it someone's*
job to speak for us & now & now; what light bares in us.

∞

If starlight be waves in carry through space; say *speed of light in a vacuum*; how a country moves with the voices of its people on its back; how we carried by misdeeds in a justice system that sees color & distastes it, sees the poor under its gavel & wields despite, blindfold long removed moons ago, scales in twist in distort.

∞

If starlight be how you produce, charged particle, in acceleration; wave of you brings energy & momentum to give from a source to matter you interact with; how generous a source found in lungs, brain, & aortic sack; say *what makes you human makes you powerful*; let all who treat you inhumane feel your energy in pulse.

∞

If starlight be & you single photon rest in mass of zero, rest in the infinite design of a mouth open before all the numbers in the universe tumble out & become yours for the taking; linger brief, here, on the verge; do not let roles & officials wipe your name, use your trachea, your tongue to speak, lest you begin to forget.

NO APOLOGIES TO AMERICA ANYMORE

In our nation's capital

& what releases from your body being part sigh, part admission of
how *otherness* swiftly permeates, here in the marble & brass, stone
of it all; the copper smell in keep on your hands; legs hold you in
say *place* in belly of *Exploring the Early Americas*, say *exhibit* in wince,
in cellular reaction; you find yourself in exhibition; you find a tight
heart in harsh constriction; your eyes in languid repose upon face
of stranger, of stranger, & stranger still; the history inside you,
coded & writhing out of dormant only a deep burrow of, say *self-
preservation distresses*; how you always & never Mexican until
moments of now, in front of "The Sad Night," in roil of oils red
after Moctezuma's death; how Library states, *drama of the encounters
between Native Americans and European explorers*, as if simple & show
& spectacle; act of us taken from; think *genocide* & turn, in hollow.

Poem to America

Grit under nails, belly of food stamps & government cheese: see, this body constructed in poverty, under the fists of many, who you taught to fear for her own Latina skin, who grew inside your guts—no longer a child's throat, spine elongates behind trachea, strength of bone, & yes, say *vocal cords*, say *what haunts you now*: singular voices, in collect.

In preparation for fiery climates: a poem to America

Gag orders; you at the window, how both in stiff, in resistance; pressure applies; frigid air burrows throat to lungs, in elicitation of burn; this fiery climate cores you; here, at open window, you find yourself; this desire to jumpstart & all elements comprise— think *flesh first*, stroke your collarbone—all these curved edges, say *body me of*, think *sentient tethers you to other*; how do we align anything so vast as cellular, immense as consciousness; we stroke our misconstrued infinities, how we forget *finite* inside *infinite*; we carve the question on the undersides of muscle, striations in envelop & envelop until we bellies full from the taste of ourselves & we forget answers etch there too; say *inside first* & how we ready again; how we make cycles unnatural things; if you trace a circle long enough it rolls away from you; & you left in gape of circumference, in stun.

Poem to America

Heart of you: chant *people, people, people, people, people, people* . . .

Loose clench

To prepare, elements around the heart constrict, a pulling in; how a body knows before the brain & this cage, too, for impulses, synapses, this sending & receiving of; how we trick ourselves, say *belief* & mean it; throat in feel of its own hollowness, crowds in, just so; to imbibe, we host, we aggregate; let us rend tissues, collect our molecular weight to mold anew; think *what leaving looks like*, think *your hands in gentle no longer to*; oh, the *to* the *to*; how erasure beings in untraceable acts; this hip redacted, this spine redacted, our foreheads in delicate press redacted, kitchen sonatas while making enchiladas redacted, close breath in hold of your name redacted; to strike from, to block out, this undoing of what made you, once; think *whole*, think *what now pocks away*; say *this loose clench* in teeter.

Mathematics of healing: a poem to America

Yes, the gape of wounds exists & yet how wounds elevate both
flesh & mind, transform to causeways, making us stony; so much
to harden from; today the rehab office speaks to you in costs,
addiction held up against the window for all to see & what light
shows through: the familiar symbol of capitalism, say *$ $ $* & you
weigh your partner's health against a price, a price the weight of
your heart in sag, a price that makes you speak in equations; say
price greater than your current mortgage, say *if I cannot afford do I love still*;
how some systems wrench us; & what of systems in manipulation,
of numbers never adding up; say *O healthcare O*, say *capitalism
for whom*, say *freedom—& what of afford*; a nation overjoyed to make you
poverty-bound, environmentally sick, an addict; & what of healing;
our nation offers that too, if your pockets run just deep enough.

Poem to America

An equation:

Top 1% income = 25 x Bottom 99% income (combined).

When a word breaks, who mends it; say *capitalism*; 1% benefit from the rupture.

What of you, child in learn

& what of truth, dissected out with pieces in pluck, in discard; what
of the *what we think we knows*; in this week, you read of children's
protests of Dr. Seuss's birthday; you see his cartoons, say *cartoons*
depicting Africans & African-Americans as monkeys, drawn
property; say *cartoons*, outlines depicting Japanese & Japanese-
Americans as evil saboteurs in World War II; think *how many copies of*
Oh, The Places You'll Go! *gifted to graduates*; think *O the bookshelves
containing* One Fish, Two Fish, Red Fish, Blue Fish; how history
tethers to dominance, to privilege & our image of *hero* vivid, until
what reveals; say *how truth in the missing*; only pieces of a whole; how
we fold the drawing to hide the blemish; folded from; & what of
his museum doors in open; what of concealment; what story to tell;
what of truth & the truth-teller's faults; what of you, child in learn?

In our nation's capital

Youth in shout, in poems from stone steps where *Dedicated to Art* carves the archway; think *how appropriate this school here*; metal lions forever encased in their sleep-sprawl as you cross 17th; how you in route & night's haze ripples the moon out & out, on precipice to horizon; in hesitant gait, you skim the belly of the President's Park; how your shoulders agitate, just so, & you & a biker & your lover hover on the gated path, in glimpse of the house; how distance you have become; how glow of light today pales resemblance to glow of light on January 19, the meaning of *country* before November 7; how your arms lack ability, lack reach; think *camera, no, not,* to document *this & now* builds bile in the back of your throat; where we all arrive at spectacle, where air drowns a collective decision; nothing here to—*capture*, if only a deep regret; to let go, to bolster.

Poem to America

Say *be just.*

In our nation's capital or *America is a poem*

In 1844, Emerson wrote, *America is a poem in our eyes*; neck in cock, you stand amid the busts of poets, dead white males, who still influence even this line, this attempt; you read these words rolled in paint on the wall of the Smithsonian's Portrait Museum; pupils imbibe the lavish frames, the faces in bronze, the historical testosterone in linger still; down the hall, Harriet Tubman's portrait suspends in black & white, commissioned in 1885, no larger than a family photo you may have found in your grandmother's cedar chest you used to rummage with innocent hands, with consumed curiosity; here, again, thoughts in roil; what really intrigues you, just left of Emerson's words: a crack in the museum's wall; disruption of foundation; how necessary this gesture in close proximity to, say *poetry*; you return to Tubman's photo, touch frame, retinas in write.

Poem to America

Our joints load with definitions; let's be clear, let us say the word *just* out loud, as a country, as a community, & mean: *rightful, equitable, proper*; & hold each up, into light.

Unapologetic

To you, dearest stranger, dearest amygdala, dearest burn in chest
in production of—say *yes, you know the sensation*, flap & desire to stow
in the underside of breeze, carry, say *away from fight*; how you bind
in cells, in impulses & your brain all electrical & you, conductor,
producer of—let's be clear, no apologies to America anymore; you
no longer in hyber- & the word *nation* a sore on lip's underside &
you, in tongue in tongue; velocity of pain; enormity of heal; how
humanity & *equity* redact so simply from motions the jaws crank
apart, together, apart; say *way of things now—no, you have a hand in it
all*; how brave outside the self you must be; say *uterus apologizes no
more*, say *Latina veins apologize no more*, say *clitoris apologizes no more*, say
these features that offend apologize no more, say *oh, country, the weight of doors
in close flays your heart* & all hearts inside indigenous or immigrant;
now plead with your lungs, *country, oh, country, hear our voices, ignited.*

Poem to America

Isthmus of the fauces—*passage & passage & passage.*

What haunts you now

Each morning you wake to a new song playing in your head; song fills you with remembrance, with history, with possibility of voice; do not keep voice hidden inside your skull; how you ready in chest; how the word *just* on your lips, how the word *love* lingers too: child in dive from a fingernail moon; above all, love haunts you now; how the presence of love found in most delicate places: your mother's hand upon your shoulder saying *how to see you now*, plump pucker of your partner's mouth before kiss, Goosie's hair below your chin after her first basketball game, sunlight in a ripe sky full of winged recital; & what of where love lacks; what of *not for you* decisions against, say *basic human rights*; what of racism & misogyny in govern of offices, yet not our hearts, not our heads; say *Capitol Hill be voice of all your people, be just*; in haunt, you must be voice, must.

Poem to America

You fracture: boulders
in our jaws, we here,
in your throat, climbing;
be ladder to voices; hear
us speak in you, as you.

INFINITE DESIGN OF A MOUTH, OPEN

A method for survival

No pause for season; no halt in the irreversible
succession of events, say *always just time, time,*

time; how we weavers in an immense web in
string from Milky Way to Himalayas to aspen

branches in bud, say *our plot*, to the Statue of
Liberty to this thought too upon the page; &

a deep turn exists in us, compass carved behind
the breast bone; born in rhythms we (r)evolve

in a planet that alludes the immense silence of
space, a planet in gentle tilt toward the burn of

a star; subjects of light, subjects of sound left
to our own fumblings; organs of hearing, say

drums, O drums, in stimulation of vibration; how
we spider legs, how we caught in our own; how

the spider speaks in silk, mouth of webs; how
one gossamer filament floats from our jaws,

agape at the sky, say *what awe in open*; & throat
a tunnel, a shuttle in, a shuttle out; & what

conjures in the realm of larynx, lungs in respire;
say *let us spell voice, let us expel voice*: a type of

magic; how this fine-spun float becomes sky of
cobwebs: a method for entrapment, say *snare of*

our shadows, or a method for survival, say *just say.*

Ghost of innocence

On the couch, labored breath of whiskey, chest
in spasmodic heave, his feet still in steel-toed

work boots; & a slow unlace of each boot with
gentleness you didn't know you still possess—

no *ask* for this exists, no written rules on, say
an addict's anything, say *motives*, as if to rationalize

baffling; you sit next to him in the chair & cell
phone scrolls headlines of cuts: cuts of NEA

cuts of EPA, cuts of healthcare; you fall back
into old fabric & pillows & absorb the gravity

of words: *baffle, president, addict*; you imagine a
body so weightless, a whole nation floats away.

& in unmake, reveal

Lull out of winter now, out of barren, out of
battered—scores of melodies reside in you,

in belly beyond light of pupil tunnels; speak to
cavities between organs & vessels; speak to

nerve impulses in thread of you; say *be done now*
with this hiding inside bone, this chisel only

inward; how you hollow in—*enough now*; step
out into a nation where injured voices burrow

out; feel your own throat there, in heal in long
mend from deep wounds; the unmake of; look

around you the palms of other in reach & your
own hands in release of fists, splay, ready for.

& of heart & home America

Bind your heart with string, wrap over wrap
until lines imprint a new pattern to trace dull

& allow for no more swell, no more rupture,
no more arrows in shape of words & your chest

a collapsible target; let you be done
with the practice of forgetting; let you close

ventricles to the dust of a nation's illness,
sickness of; how *hate* malevolent out of letters;

& malevolent out of skin; in you hatch voice,
one of a house sparrow, one of songs & alarms;

make you sparrow by definition to home:
home your body sings for & prides to protect.

Poem for you, America

Yes, we here together on this crumbling ridge,
my hand a ligature in your palm & you in tug,

in pull from my breasts & estrogen, my brown
flesh; my veins continue into your veins & one

tear, tears us both to bleed; & yet you whine,
you scramble & so much wounds; what you

don't know is this weathering of me shall pass
& these ventricles in me, pumping organs &

impulses to transmit thought, feed you; say *319
million palms*, appendages, circulate you & brutal

& hateful, sickens you; we stand in a sun-swept
horizon, a raw dawn, in demand of justice.

& in mend, we

We live in systems of hydrogen, systems of oxygen, systems of nitrogen; O compounds in thrust of a universe in dare to dream of; think *how human of you*; your elements remember wombing in the dark of galaxy just before; what binds you in these systems of calcium, systems of vessels, systems of proteins?

∞

A body's mass mostly water; say *O composition, O organ of*; what nervous tissues synapse throughout, say *us*, say *thought deepens us*; element constituent to whole, how in chemistry, the substance of class unable to separate into simpler, into means in vast combination connect, intimately so; what necessity, what life.

∞

We live in correlation to our naturalness on a planet; say *Earth, yes, a system &*
what of our desire to control; we live in web to the unnatural strokes of society;
strokes created by our system to create systems first to organize, to understand,
& then to dominate; what of this motion, say *power*, taken in haste, in greed?

∞

& active toxics also dwell within the body; trace amounts of lead & arsenic & bromine; what composes us; what makes us human also makes us slivers of deadly; say *poison in higher amounts*; this justification of; how cells in us: bacteria cells in reside of our gastrointestinal tract; how wondrously not human at all.

∞

The body in host, in love with its own guests; body demonstrates generosity despite harsh treatment; & of systems in circulation without care or love for you; systems that deteriorate you: societies, nations, rules built not for you, not for your ovaries, not your Latina blood, not your poverty, not your heart.

∞

How you think of your liver, of detoxification, in tuck under the right ribs above the belly, meaty organ; what requires the liver's functions, lobules, cells metabolizing in strain from what the body endures; so much in burn inside you; this, above all, is a love story; this, above all, a system that loves you more.

∞

& what of horrid histories, of our young black bodies dying in streets, of our gay teens beaten & tied to posts, of incarceration as a loophole for slavery, of atrocities to women legitimized by a president who says, *grab them by the pussy*; how we must proceed in the weight of broken, of battered, of loathsome.

∞

& of the systems that do not love, obvious & broken; how they unravel what
we think we know; fray our thoughts until a new form of measurement exists;
& the brave not unlike the liver, delicate & secreting, fight for less toxicity;
here too, a love story forms amid the bile; how we always in mend of, mending.

∞

In our assemblage we marvel to see faces of family, of strangers, of friends, of vaguely familiar, & our own face; we all borne under the same sun with same organic impulses in transmit throughout our membranes, dendrites, muscles; our same spark of being; none of which the lesser; O lovely existence in share.

∞

& who built this system; how far to stray, how far to go; & we must shelf fear,
let voice tend to us, let voice rise from intersection of mind & heart & lungs;
call out systems of hate; call out systems that once made may now be unmade;
let us be makers of a new nation, new home, new accountable thought.

∞

Let us speak of systems; let us speak of all that gate & limit our humanity; let our speech transform a list into a litany, one that opens sky to rain full-beating hearts upon the heartless & we all be doused in the *thump, thump, thump* of affection & lean our skeletal structures closer to share in rhythm made new.

About the Author

Felicia Zamora's books include *Of Form & Gather*, the 2016 Andrés Montoya Poetry Prize winner, *Instrument of Gaps*, and *& in Open, Marvel*. A 2019 CantoMundo fellow, she won the 2015 Tomaž Šalamun Prize and was the 2017 Poet Laureate of Fort Collins, CO. Her poems appear in *Academy of American Poets* (Poem-A-Day), the *Georgia Review*, the *Missouri Review* (Poem of the Week), the *Nation*, and others. She is the associate poetry editor for *Colorado Review*, holds an MFA from Colorado State University, and is the program manager for the Center for Imagination in the Borderlands at Arizona State University. She lives in Phoenix, Arizona with her partner Chris and their two dogs.